THE KNOWLEDGE
OF
GOOD AND EVIL

by Dr. James McKeever

This booklet is dedicated
first and foremost
to the glory of God
and of His Son, Jesus Christ.

THE KNOWLEDGE OF GOOD AND EVIL

Printed in the United States of America
First Printing April, 1981
Second Printing May, 1989

Omega Publications
P. O. Box 4130
Medford, Oregon 97501 U.S.A.

Special rates for bulk orders and for bookstores.

ISBN 0-86694-084-7

THE KNOWLEDGE OF GOOD AND EVIL

There are some bedrock foundational truths of the Christian faith that seem to be neglected nowadays. Two of these that the Lord has laid strongly on my heart are published in booklets. ONLY ONE WORD deals with the first and great commandment to love God with all of our heart, soul and mind.

Another booklet, WHY WERE YOU CREATED?, similarly deals with one of these bedrock issues. Many Christians don't know why they were created, so how could they possibly be doing, to the best of their ability, what they were created to do?

Here I want to write on a third bedrock foundational truth that I have rarely seen taught. It deals with the first commandment given to man; therefore, God must have thought it was very important. It was the prohibition against gaining knowledge of good and evil. It has far more implications than one might realize, so stay with us as we go back and review the two special trees in the garden of Eden.

4 This is the account of the heavens and the earth when they were created, in the day that the LORD God made earth and heaven.
5 Now no shrub of the field was yet in the earth, and no plant of the field had yet sprouted, for the LORD God had not sent rain upon the earth; and there was no man to cultivate the ground.

3

6 But a mist used to rise from the earth and water the whole surface of the ground.

7 Then the LORD God formed man of dust from the ground, and breathed into his nostrils the breath of life; and man became a living being.

8 And the LORD God planted a garden toward the east, in Eden; and there He placed the man whom He had formed.

9 And out of the ground the LORD God caused to grow every tree that is pleasing to the sight and good for food, the tree of life also in the midst of the garden, and the tree of the knowledge of good and evil.

—Genesis 2

As we can see in this passage, there were many trees of all kinds in the garden of Eden. But there were two special trees:

1. The tree of life
2. The tree of the knowledge of good and evil

As we all know, God forbade Adam and Eve to eat of the tree of the knowledge of good and evil, as is recorded further in Genesis 2:

15 Then the LORD God took the man and put him into the garden of Eden to cultivate it and keep it.

16 And the LORD God commanded the man, saying, "From any tree of the garden you may eat freely;

17 but from the tree of the knowledge of good and evil you shall not eat, for in the day that you eat from it you shall surely die."

It is interesting that they were not forbidden to eat of the tree of life. It is possible that they ate regularly from the tree of life. Perhaps that is one of the reasons they lived to be almost one thousand years old.

4

In Genesis 3 we find God casting Adam and Eve out of the garden so that they could not longer eat of the tree of life.

22 Then the LORD God said, "Behold, the man has become like one of Us, knowing good and evil; and now lest he stretch out his hand, and take also from the tree of life, and eat, and live forever"—

23 therefore the LORD God sent him out from the garden of Eden, to cultivate the ground from which he was taken.

24 So He drove the man out; and at the east of the garden of Eden he stationed the cherubim, and the flaming sword which turned every direction, to guard the way to the tree of life.

—Genesis 3

The reason God no longer wanted them to eat of the tree of life is because they had gained something God never wanted them to have—the knowledge of good and evil.

The fall of Adam and Eve involved much more than the sin of disobeying God. Because of that sin, they gained the knowledge of good and evil. If gaining the knowledge of good and evil was such a terrible thing that God cast them out of the garden, we need to understand why it was so bad and find out if it is also bad for you and me.

YOU CAN KNOW GOD OR GOOD AND EVIL, BUT NOT BOTH

I have first stated the conclusion—"you can know God or good and evil, but not both"—and would now like to present the evidence for it. This is a fairly bold statement that requires a close examination.

Before they ate of the forbidden fruit of the tree of knowledge of good and evil, Adam and Eve could make decisions such as naming the animals, but for any moral decision, they had to go ask God. Evidently He walked frequently in the garden of Eden, and any questions they had concerning what was right or wrong, good or bad, they simply asked God and He told them.

He did not want them making their own moral judgments as to what was good and evil based on their own knowledge. This is the reason that He prohibited them from eating of that particular tree. Satan in the worst way wanted to break this relationship of dependence upon God, as we see recorded in Chapter 3 of Genesis:

1 Now the serpent was more crafty than any beast of the field which the LORD God had made. And he said to the woman, "Indeed, has God said, 'You shall not eat from any tree of the garden'?"

2 And the woman said to the serpent, "From the fruit of the trees of the garden we may eat;

3 but from the fruit of the tree which is in the middle of the garden, God has said, 'You shall not eat from it or touch it, lest you die.'"

4 And the serpent said to the woman, "You surely shall not die.

5 "For God knows that in the day you eat from it your eyes will be opened, and you will be like God, knowing good and evil."

6 When the woman saw that the tree was good for food, and that it was a delight to the eyes, and that the tree was desirable to make one wise, she took from its fruit and ate; and she gave also to her husband with her, and he ate.

7 Then the eyes of both of them were opened, and they knew that they were naked; and they sewed fig leaves together and made themselves loin coverings.

8 And they heard the sound of the LORD God walking in the garden in the cool of the day, and the man and his wife hid themselves from the presence of the LORD God among the trees of the garden.

9 Then the LORD God called to the man, and said to him, "Where are you?"

10 And he said, "I heard the sound of Thee in the garden, and I was afraid because I was naked; so I hid myself."

11 And He said, "Who told you that you were naked? Have you eaten from the tree of which I commanded you not to eat?"

—Genesis 3

Adam and Eve had been naked from the beginning, and evidently neither they nor God had seen anything wrong with it. However, once they ate of the tree of the knowledge of good and evil, Adam and Eve realized they were naked and concluded that it was wrong. They then made themselves aprons of leaves to cover their nakedness.

When God came into the garden, He called them out from their hiding place. I can just imagine Him asking them where they got those silly clothes, and Adam and Eve responding that they had made them. God might have asked, "Why did you make them? Why did you hide yourself?" and Adam would have replied, "Because I was naked." I imagine that God might have responded, "So what?" Then Adam must have said, "But that is wrong."

God must have wept inside as He asked them who told them they were naked and what made them think it was wrong. He already must have known the answer, but then He asked them if they had eaten of the tree of the knowledge of good and evil.

Before Adam and Eve ate the fruit of the tree of the knowledge of good and evil, when they had to make a moral decision they went to God, and they did whatever He said. After they ate of it, they could use their own knowledge, reasoning and feelings about what was right and wrong to make all of these decisions, independent of God. Either Adam and Eve could make their decisions based on knowing God and what He told them to do in each specific situation, or they could make decisions based on their knowledge of good and evil, but they couldn't do both. They had chosen to rely on their own knowledge and therefore were cast out of the garden, away from the presence of God and basically away from the guidance of God. Actually, it was because of

His mercy that God cast them out of the garden, away from the tree of life, because He didn't want them to live forever in their sinful state, relying on their own knowledge instead of on Him.

You could state the principle in this way:

Knowing God and knowing good and evil are mutually exclusive.

God's desire that man not adopt a knowledge of good and evil did not change with the new covenant. We are exhorted to discern good and evil (Hebrews 5:14), but discernment is a spiritual matter and not a matter of the mind. Since we, as Christians, are indwelt with the Holy Spirit, we have access to His discernment as to that which is right or wrong in our lives or in our surroundings. However, this is very much different than *knowledge* of good and evil, which would rely on the use of our mind. Thus, the *knowledge* of good and evil amount to leaning on our own understanding, whereas the *discernment* of good and evil relies instead on the Holy Spirit. We must listen to the Holy Spirit (for discernment) and not our minds (for knowledge).

13 "But woe to you, scribes and Pharisees, hypocrites, because you shut off the kingdom of heaven from men; for you do not enter in yourselves, nor do you allow those who are entering to go in.

14 "Woe to you, scribes and Pharisees, hypocrites, because you devour widows' houses, even while for a pretense you make long prayers; therefore you shall receive grater condemnation.

15 "Woe to you, scribes and Pharisees, hypocrites, because you travel about on sea and land to make one proselyte, and when he becomes one, you make him twice as much a son of hell as yourselves. . . .

23 Woe to you, scribes and Pharisees, hypocrites! For you tithe mint and dill and cummin, and have neglected the weightier provisions of the law; justice

and mercy and faithfulness; but these are the things you should have done without neglecting the others. . . .

25 "Woe to you, scribes and Pharisees, hypocrites! For you clean the outside of the cup and of the dish, but inside they are full of robbery and self-indulgence.
26 "You blind Pharisee, first clean the inside of the cup and of the dish, so that the outside of it may become clean also.
27 "Woe to you, scribes and Pharisees, hypocrites! For you are like whitewashed tombs which on the outside appear beautiful, but inside they are full of dead men's bones and all uncleanness. . . .

37 "O Jerusalem, Jerusalem, who kills the prophets and stones those who are sent to her! How often I wanted to gather your children together the way a hen gathers her chicks under her wings, and you were unwilling. . . ."
—Matthew 23

As we can see, Christ condemned the Pharisees who did everything according to their knowledge of good and evil. They were not close to God, did not hear God, and even rejected God's very own Son.

In verse 37 of Matthew 23, Christ cries out to the inhabitants of Jerusalem, yearning to gather them in a loving way as a hen gathers her chicks, yearning to reestablish this personal relationship. But they were so enslaved to their knowledge of good and evil that they could not have a personal relationship with God through His Son, Jesus Christ.

A strong teaching on this subject is found in Proverbs 3:

5 Trust in the Lord with all your heart,
    And do not lean on your own understanding.
6 In all your ways acknowledge Him,
    And He will make your paths straight.

In these verses it says that if we do three things, then God will guide us (make our paths straight). It says we are to:

1. Trust in the Lord with all our heart.
2. Lean not to our own understanding.
3. In all our ways acknowledge Him.

If we do those three things, then He promises that He will guide us or the King James Version says, "and He shall direct thy paths." The second of these requirements is by far the hardest. It is that we do not lean to our understanding, and I believe this means our understanding of what is good and evil, or right and wrong. The smarter an individual is, the more difficult this is for him. But the strong implication is that you can either have God guide your paths *or* you can lean to your own understanding, but you cannot do both.

A lot of churches teach things like "do not handle this," "Do not taste that," "Do not touch the other." This kind of instruction is based on their knowledge of good and evil, which they try to impose upon their members. These people mean well, but they forget what Colossians 2 says on this:

> **20 If you have died with Christ to the elementary principles of the world, why, as if you were living in the world, do you submit yourself to decrees, such as**
> **21 "Do not handle, do not taste, do not touch!"**
> **22 (which all refer to things destined to perish with the using)—in accordance with the commandments and teachings of men?**
> **23 These are matters which have, to be sure, the appearance of wisdom in self-made religion and self-abasement and severe treatment of the body, but are of no value against fleshly indulgence.**
> **—Colossians 2**

As we can see from these verses, having these lists of "do's" and "don'ts" gives an appearance of wisdom but the Bible says they are of no value against fleshly indulgence. In other words, the knowledge of good and evil will never keep us from sinning and indulging in things of the flesh. Knowing God and having a close personal relationship with Him will keep us from indulging in these fleshly things. So once again we see that knowing God and knowing good and evil are mutually exclusive.

KNOWLEDGE OF GOOD AND EVIL
CAN PREVENT US FROM OBEYING GOD

It is interesting to note that our knowledge of good and evil can cause us to sin (sin being disobedience to God). This sounds like an incredible statement, but put yourself in the place of Abraham. What if God told you to go out and kill or sacrifice your only or your favorite child? Most of us would argue with God and say, "But God, that is wrong." Our knowledge of good and evil would prevent us from obeying God.

It is not only our knowledge of good and evil that can keep us from obeying God; it is also our logical mind (which perhaps is just another facet of the knowledge of good and evil). For example, Abraham was living in the Ur of the Chaldees in a very luxurious home. This home has been excavated and it was a two-story brick home, which one can visit today if one can get into Iraq. He had a very comfortable life and was evidently very content when God told him to pack up everything and to "Go West, young man," to a land that He would show him. Abraham didn't even know where he was going, nor how he would get there, nor how he would recognize it when he arrived.

To many of Abraham's friends, I'm sure this was a stupid, illogical and insane thing to do. God frequently asks us to do things that don't seem logical or that seem to violate our sense of what is right and wrong. Many people, had they been in Abraham's situation, would have allowed their knowledge of good and evil to prevent them from leaving their plush homes, businesses and surroundings to become nomads living in tents. You might even ask yourself the question, if God asked you right now to leave everything you own, taking a minimum of possessions, to start moving north or south, and to live in a tent, what would you do?

Baptism is an interesting example of what we are discussing. If someone stands up in front of a church and publicly declares that he has received Jesus Christ as his Savior, there is absolutely no logical reason to be baptized. I believe that at the very beginning of our Christian life God asks us to do something that is illogical and to do it simply because He asks us to. This is to prepare us so that when He later asks us to do very difficult things that are illogical, we will be used to obeying.

God has asked me to do a number of highly illogical things. As I was zooming up the IBM management ladder, He said: "Take a year's leave of absence and go live on Catalina Island in a cove, where there is no electricity or telephones, and no roads into the place, and be a caretaker at a camp." I did this, and God tremendously blessed it. Later, I was living in Los Angeles and God told me to move to Canada. There was no logical reason to move to Canada but I did, and there I found my wife, Jeani. I am absolutely convinced that He took me to Canada just to find her. Many Christians would have allowed their logical reasoning and their knowledge of good and evil to prevent them from obeying God in these and many similar situations.

You might say: "But Abraham was before the Ten Commandments. God asked him to sacrifice his son before the commandment 'thou shalt not kill' was given." All right, let's take a look at what happened after the Ten Commandments were given in Exodus 20. We find this recorded in Exodus 32, after Moses came back down from the mountain:

22   And Aaron said, "Do not let the anger of my lord burn; you know the people yourself, that they are prone to evil.

23   "For they said to me, 'Make a god for us who will go before us; for this Moses, the man who brought us up from the land of Egypt, we do not know what has become of him.'

24 "And I said to them, 'Whoever has any gold, let them tear it off.' So they gave it to me, and I threw it into the fire, and out came this calf."

25 Now when Moses saw that the people were out of control—for Aaron had let them get out of control to be a derision among their enemies—

26 then Moses stood in the gate of the camp, and said, "Whoever is for the Lord, come to me!" And all the sons of Levi gathered together to him.

27 And he said to them, "Thus says the Lord, the God of Israel, 'Every man of you put his sword upon his thigh, and go back and forth from gate to gate in the camp, and kill every man his brother, and every man his friend, and every man his neighbor.'"

28 So the sons of Levi did as Moses instructed, and about three thousand men of the people fell that day.

29 Then Moses said, "Dedicate yourselves today to the Lord—for every man has been against his son and against his brother—in order that He may bestow a blessing upon you today."

—Exodus 32

Had you been there and had you been a son of Levi (part of the priesthood), would you have strapped on your sword and gone out, under God's command, to kill all those who were sinning by worshiping the calf, whether they be your brother, your friend, or your neighbor? That is what the sons of Levi did. Many Christians living in the United States today would have refused to obey God because their "knowledge of good and evil" would have told them that it was wrong.

LESSONS FROM ELIJAH

We might excuse Moses and the sons of Levi from these types of acts. Perhaps even Joshua. God told him to go into a town and kill everyone, including the old women and babies even one day old. Our knowledge of good and evil would have caused most of us to refuse to be a part of it. The same would be true of the victorious time at Jericho, when God

13

caused the walls to fall down. Every one of God's children there went forward into the city over the crumbled walls and, at God's command, killed all of those in the city; Rehab the harlot and those who were with her in her house were the only ones left alive. You might discount this because Joshua was the military leader of his people. That's true, but he was under marching orders from God.

So let's go to a man we would all consider a true prophet and a man of God, Elijah. No doubt we have all studied and rejoiced in the fact that Elijah had the contest with 450 of Baal's prophets, and that God honored him by bringing fire down from heaven and consuming the sacrifice, the wood, and even the water in the trench. All rejoiced in God's power and victory. But we tend to stop before the end of the story:

> **22 Then Elijah said to the people, "I alone am left a prophet of the LORD, but Baal's prophets are 450 men. . . ."**
>
> **36 Then it came about at the time of the offering of the evening sacrifice, that Elijah the prophet came near and said, "O LORD, the God of Abraham, Isaac and Israel, today let it be known that Thou art God in Israel, and that I am Thy servant, and that I have done all these things at Thy word.**
>
> **37 "Answer me, O LORD, answer me, that this people may know that Thou, O LORD, art God, and that Thou has turned their heart back again."**
>
> **38 Then the fire of the Lord fell, and consumed the burnt offering and the wood and the stones and the dust, and licked up the water that was in the trench. . . .**
>
> **40 Then Elijah said to them, "Seize the prophets of Baal, do not let one of them escape." So they seized them; and Elijah brought them down to the brook Kishon, and slew them there.**
>
> **—1 Kings 18**

At the end of the story Elijah had to kill the false prophets of Baal. It is all part of the story. Many of us would love to have been there and prayed and seen the fire come down from heaven, but likely, because of our knowledge of good and evil, we would have refused to have killed the 450 false prophets of Baal. Perhaps that is why we do not have the power of God like Elijah did, because we want to selectively obey God based on our own knowledge of good and evil.

Let's track further and see another significant event in the life of Elijah:

9   Then the king sent to him a captain of fifty with his fifty.   And he went up to him, and behold, he was sitting on the top of the hill.   And he said to him, "O man of God, the king says, 'Come down.'"

10   And Elijah answered and said to the captain of fifty, "If I am a man of God, let fire come down from heaven and consume you and your fifty."   Then fire came down from heaven and consumed him and his fifty.

11   So he again sent to him another captain of fifty with his fifty.   And he answered and said to him, "O man of God, thus says the king, 'Come down quickly.'"

12   And Elijah answered and said to them, "If I am a man of God, let fire come down from heaven and consume you and your fifty."   Then the fire of God came down from heaven and consumed him and his fifty.

13   So he again sent the captain of a third fifty with his fifty.   When the third captain of fifty went up, he came and bowed down on his knees before Elijah, and begged him and said to him, "O man of God, please let my life and the lives of these fifty servants of yours be precious in your sight.

14   "Behold fire came down from heaven, and consumed the first two captains of fifty with their fifties; but now let my life be precious in your sight."

15   And the angel of the Lord said to Elijah, "Go down with him; do not be afraid of him." So he arose and went down with him to the king.

—2 Kings 1

Here, on two occasions, we see Elijah calling down fire from heaven and destroying a captain and his 50 men. So in this passage, Elijah killed, under the orders of God and by the power of God, 102 men, in addition to the 450 he had killed earlier. We normally do not think of a man of God, a prophet, in this kind of a role.

If God had led us twice to bring down fire and destroy opposing armies, most of us would have "assumed" that God wanted us to do the same thing again when we saw the third group of 50 coming toward us. So we would have called down fire and destroyed them. But Elijah, a real man of God, was listening to God on every occasion, and the third time God said to do exactly the opposite; He said to go with them. Again, perhaps this is why we do not have the power of Elijah had. God will only give that kind of power to people who, on every occasion, will walk sensitive to the leading of the Holy Spirit.

You may think: "Well, this was all in the Old Testament. Nothing like this would ever occur in the New Testament." I would like to take two examples from the New Testament. The first one fits right in with what we have been discussing about Elijah. It is found in Revelation 11:

3 "And I will grant authority to my two witnesses, and they will prophesy for twelve hundred and sixty days, clothed in sackcloth."
4 These are the two olive trees and the two lampstands that stand before the Lord of the earth.
5 And if anyone desire to harm them, fire proceeds out of their mouth and devours their enemies; and if anyone would desire to harm them, in this manner he must be killed.
6 These have the power to shut up the sky; in order that rain may not fall during the days of their prophesying; and they have power over the waters to turn them into blood, and to smite the earth with every plague, as often as they desire.

Here we see that God is again going to give the kind of power that Elijah had; the two witnesses (and I believe that is two witness companies, not two individuals) will have power to call fire down from heaven to destroy their enemies. Unfortunately, most Christians could miss becoming part of the two witness companies because their knowledge of good and evil would prevent them from calling fire down from heaven to destroy their enemies, if God were to ask them to do such a thing.

Let me hasten to reaffirm that in no way am I for killing. I hate it. I would hate to be forced to do it. What I am saying is that I want to be willing to obey my God *whatever* He tells me to do in the turbulent times ahead.

I have taken many of these examples involving killing as an *extreme* illustration of the principle to help you realize the significance of what we are talking about. Now let's turn to an example that might be more likely for many people to experience:

1 "**Then the kingdom of heaven will be comparable to ten virgins, who took their lamps, and went out to meet the bridegroom.**
2 "**And five of them were foolish, and five were prudent.**
3 "**For when the foolish took their lamps, they took no oil with them,**
4 **but the prudent took oil in flasks along with their lamps.**
5 "**Now while the bridegroom was delaying, they all got drowsy and began to sleep.**
6 "**But at midnight there was a shout, 'Behold the bridegroom! Come out to meet him.'**
7 "**Then all those virgins rose, and trimmed their lamps.**
8 "**And the foolish said to the prudent, 'Give us some of your oil, for our lamps are going out.'**

9   "But the prudent answered, saying, 'No, there will not be enough for us and you too; go instead to the dealers and buy some for yourselves.'

10   "And while they were going away to make the purchase, the bridegroom came, and those who were ready went in with him to the wedding feast; and the door was shut.

11   "And later the other virgins also came, saying, 'Lord, Lord, open up for us.'

12   "But He answered and said, 'Truly I say to you, I do not know you.'

13   "Be on the alert then, for you do not know the day nor the hour. . . ."

—Matthew 25

If most Christians today were one of the five virgins who had surplus oil, and the other five virgins who had run out of oil came to us, we would think that the "Christian thing to do" would be to share our surplus oil with them. This concept is based on our knowledge of good and evil. However, as Christ teaches, in this instance, it would have been sin for the five wise virgins, who had prepared ahead and brought extra oil, to have shared their oil with the foolish ones, who had made no preparation. Here once more we can see that our knowledge of good and evil would have caused us to sin. It is difficult to think of sharing as a sin, but anything we do can be sin if it isn't what God is telling us to do.

In times of crisis ahead, God may have led you to prepare by storing extra food, water or oil. If He tells you to share, *praise God*! Give some or all of it away, as He directs. If He tells you not to share, then don't do it. We must take our orders directly from Him and not make our decisions based on our knowledge of good and evil.

We could take many other examples from both the Old and New Testaments. It would have been sin for Noah to let additional people into the ark, even though they were dying and pounding on the door. On the other hand, it would have been sin for the widow lady (and her son) *not* to share the flour and oil with God's prophet (1 Kings 17:11-16).

We like to make little rules for ourselves, such as "it is always good to share" or "it is never good to kill." Do you see what we are doing? Once we say that we will *always* do this or we will never do that, God can no longer lead us in that area of our lives. Our well-meaning rules take precedence over God's leading.

In the Bible, there are times when it glorifies God to share and times when it is sin. There are times when God has asked one of His servants to call down fire to destroy enemies and other times when it would have been sin to do that. We cannot depend on our rules or our knowledge of good and evil. We must listen to God's voice on each occasion and do what *He* tells us to do.

YOU CAN USE THE BIBLE TO
MAKE DECISIONS INDEPENDENT OF GOD

You and I can actually use the Bible to make decisions independent of God. We can say, "The Bible says this here; therefore I will do such and such," without ever asking God what He wants. This assumes that God always wants us to do the same thing in the same set of circumstances. That may not be so. You remember the example of Elijah who twice called down fire to destroy the captains and the 50's, but the third time he did not. Instead he went with them because God told him to.

What we are saying is that some people try to make the New Testament a new law. We are no longer under the law, but we are under the Spirit and under grace (Romans 6:14; 8:2, 14).

I like to think of it this way: If I were in a car and there were speed limit signs of 55 mph all along the freeway but I were guaranteed that there were no policemen within 300 miles, I would probably go faster than 55 mph.

But if you took down all the 55 mph speed limit signs and put a policeman in the car with me and he said "Go 55," I would probably do a maximum of 54 mph.

A law is of little effect (except to show us our sin—Romans 7:7), but an indwelling Spirit can and does control us. We are no longer under the law, we are under the Spirit. This means that we live a holier and more righteous life than we would if we were under the law, so it is not an excuse for sinning. But in being under the Spirit, having a personal relationship with God, and doing what He says, there is life! Following a bunch of do's and don'ts, even those collected from the New Testament, is death.

The main emphasis of Christ's life was not on keeping the law, but on saying what the Father told Him to say and doing what the Father told Him to do—and believe me, there *is* a difference. In fact, you can make a pretty good case that Christ broke the Ten Commandments, specifically the one about keeping the Sabbath (Exodus 16:29; Luke 6:1-5) and the one about honoring your father and mother (Matthew 12:46-50; John 2:1-4; Matthew 10:34-37). Christ did come to do His Father's will:

> **38 "For I have come down from heaven, not to do My own will, but the will of Him who sent Me. . . ."**
> **—John 6**

Christ came not to do His own will, based on His knowledge of good and evil, but the will of the Father. Christ devoted His life to doing whatever God told Him to do.

If you are questioning the thought that we are not under the Ten Commandments, let me share with you what Paul says in Romans 6:

> **14 For sin shall not be master over you, for you are not under law, but under grace.**

As you can see here, the Bible says that we are no longer under the law. And to be sure that we understood which law he was talking about, in Chapter 7 of Romans, Paul then quotes one of the Ten Commandments. He wanted to be certain that we did not erroneously think that we were released from the ceremonial law of the Old Testament but were still under the Ten Commandments. Thus, he made it very clear that we are not under the law, including the Ten Commandments:

> **6 But now we have been released from the Law, having died to that by which we were bound, so that we serve in newness of the Spirit and not in oldness of the letter.**
> **7 What shall we say then? Is the Law sin? May it never be! On the contrary, I would not have come to know sin except through the Law; for I would not have known about coveting if the Law had not said, "You shall not covet."**
>
> **—Romans 7**

What I am saying is that we can use the Bible, even the Ten Commandments, to make decisions that are independent of God. Our desire, like Christ's, should be to do our Father's will. Thus, in everything and in every situation, we should ask God what His will is and then be careful to do it, even if it seems to contradict our knowledge of good and evil.

There are many other examples that we could give of Christ telling others not to do what we would consider to be "right," based on our knowledge of good and evil. If someone were going to follow Christ, but his father had just died, we would think that the "right" thing to do would be to go bury his father first, and then follow Jesus. But Jesus commanded the opposite and refused to let a man go to his father's funeral in Luke 9:

> **59 And He said to another, "Follow Me." But he said, "Permit me first to go and bury my father."**
> **60 But He said to him, "Allow the dead to bury their own dead; but as for you, go and proclaim everywhere the kingdom of God."**

21

61 And another also said, "I will follow You, Lord; but first permit me to say goodbye to those at home."

62 But Jesus said to him, "No one, after putting his hand to the plow and looking back is fit for the kingdom of God."

Our thinking is not His thinking, our ways are not His ways (Isaiah 55:8,9)! If I felt we were still under the Ten Commandments, I would "worship" on Saturday (the Sabbath or the seventh day) and not on Sunday (the first day).

8 "Remember the sabbath day, to keep it holy.

9 "Six days you shall labor and do all your work,

10 but the seventh day is a sabbath of the LORD your God; in it you shall not do any work, you or your son or your daughter, your male or your female servant or your cattle or your sojourner who stays with you.

11 "For in six days the LORD made the heavens and the earth, the sea and all that is in them, and rested on the seventh day; therefore the LORD blessed the sabbath day and made it holy. . . ."

—Exodus 20

When a person treats Sunday, instead of Saturday, as the holy day, he is breaking the Ten Commandments. This is a fact, no matter how one might try to justify worshiping on Sunday. However, keeping Sunday holy might be God's will and what would glorify Christ.

RENEWING YOUR MIND

The first two verses of Romans 12 are two of my very favorite verses:

1 I urge you therefore, brethren, by the mercies of God, to present your bodies a living and holy sacrifice, acceptable to God, which is your spiritual service of worship.

2 And do not be conformed to this world, but be transformed by the renewing of your mind, that you

may prove what the will of God is that which is good and acceptable and perfect.

—Romans 12

Verse 2 tells us that the way we are able to present our bodies as a living sacrifice and not to be conformed to the world is *by the renewing of our minds.* It doesn't say to make our minds new. It says to *renew* our minds. Like other words that start with "re," it means to "make it like it used to be." For example, *revive* means to restore life, and *replenish* means to bring the supply back to what it was. *Renew* means to make it new like it used to be.

So we are to renew our minds, or to make them like they used to be. Make them like they used to be *when*? Like when we were babies? Like before we were Christians? Like when we were young Christians? No, no! I certainly don't want my mind renewed to one of those states! Then what is the time period to which we are to have our minds renewed? I believe that Romans 12:2 is telling us to have our minds renewed to the way they were before the fall. In what way were Adam and Eve's minds, before the fall, different from our minds?

The only difference that I can isolate is that Adam and Eve, before they sinned, did not know good and evil, and we do. If we are going to renew our minds to be like theirs were, we are going to have to put aside our knowledge of good and evil and just know God.

Lord, whatever it takes, help us to renew our minds to a state like the minds of Adam and Eve, before they sinned and gained the knowledge of good and evil, and stopped depending solely on You.

This prayer will be answered as we permit the mind of Christ, which is ours through the Holy Spirit, to take control of our lives—both in thought and deed.

DEFINITION OF SALVATION

What is your definition of salvation and eternal life? The Bible gives us a good definition in John 17:

3 "And this is eternal life, that they may know Thee, the only true God, and Jesus Christ whom Thou has sent. . ."

We can see here that the definition of eternal life is knowing God and knowing Jesus Christ, *period.* It is not a result of knowing right from wrong, good from evil; it does not come from keeping a set of rules and regulations; it is not a result of abiding by all the do's and don'ts of your church fellowship. It is in knowing God and doing His will. We study the Bible to know God better. Yet we must be careful not to use the Bible to make decisions independent of God. Every decision should be brought before the Father in prayer and then we should do whatever He tells us to do.

KNOWING GOD'S WILL

To many people, what we have shared in this booklet is scary. We are much more comfortable and secure having a set of do's and don'ts that we can follow. Realizing that in every situation we need to pray and do what God tells us to do, and that He might tell us to do different things in identical situations, leaves us with nothing to hang onto and depend on, except God.

Many people would be concerned about hearing God's voice or about how to know His will. If God cannot and does not reveal His will directly to each individual believer, then you can throw out almost the entire New Testament, because it is talking about our being under the guidance of the Holy Spirit and not under the law.

Ask yourself this question: "Is God more eager to reveal His will to me than I am to know it?" I believe that He is infinitely more eager to show you His will than you are to

24

know it. Thus, if you look up and say, "God, show me Your will," He is not going to look down and say, "Beg me," or, "Grovel a little bit and maybe I will reveal My will to you, if you beg me enough." Once He sees a Christian who is willing to do His will, whatever it is, God has absolutely no reason to withhold revealing His will and His guidance from you. He will eagerly reveal it to you in one way or another.

There are a number of ways in which God can guide you and show you His will. Of these, one is overwhelmingly the most important. We will list this most important one last, since we will deal with it last:

1. A multitude of counselors
2. Circumstances
3. The Bible
4. Direct revelation (visions, dreams or God's voice)
5. Peace in your heart

1. A multitude of counselors: Let us look at these one at a time. In this first one we are simply restating what it says in Proverbs:

> **14 Where there is guidance, the people fall,
> But in abundance of counselors there is
> victory.**
> **—Proverbs 11**

The KING JAMES VERSION says that "in the multitude of counselors there is safety." God can guide us through the counsel of others (and I would include words of personal prophecy in this category), but it should never be the counsel of just one person or even two. I would say that if this is the way that God is going to guide you, there should be counsel of a minimum of three godly, righteous men, ideally independent of each other, and not necessarily part of the same body of believers. I want to underscore that they must be *godly, righteous* men. Psalm 1 admonishes righteous men not to "walk in the counsel of the ungodly." If you are taking advice in any area of your life from a non-Christian, you are

25

walking in the counsel of the ungodly and violating what God tells you to do. I would include the financial area in this admonition. If you are taking financial advice from a non-Christian, you are violating God's commands. I would encourage you to switch and take the advice of Christians only. I think the same thing is true concerning your lawyer and CPA. These men should be Christians. If the matter is big enough, whether it be financial or legal, you should let them know that you are going to seek a "multitude of counselors." God can certainly use three or more Christian counselors to give you guidance.

2. **Circumstances:** God can use circumstances to guide us. If we are praying about going to college "A" or college "B" and college "A" rejects us and college "B" accepts us, God can use those closed doors to guide us. I emphasize *closed doors* and not open doors. I do not look at open doors as a way of God directing us, because each of us have thousands

of doors open to us every day. *The need does not constitute the call.* If we were to look at needs around the world, and even in our own community or church, where we have the ability to meet the need, we could quickly become committed to ninety-five hours a day. So I do not believe that open doors are a means that God uses to guide us. However, when God closes a door, we can rejoice in the fact that He has prevented us from doing something that wouldn't be best for us and give us the maximum happiness. Even though the door that He closes might be one that we very much wanted to walk through, we still need to praise Him for His loving care and guidance.

3. The Bible: When I say the Bible, I mean principles in the Bible and not a specific isolated verse. People have opened the Bible and read something about islands in a verse, and they took this as God calling them to be missionaries on an island. In such cases, it usually turns out to be a disaster. But even in using principles of the Bible, we have to be careful. One can use the Bible to make decisions that are independent of God. We can say to ourselves, "Well, the Bible says this; therefore, I will do it," without ever asking God what He wants us to do.

4. Direct revelation (visions, dreams or God's voice): God can guide us directly through a vision or a dream, through a visit from an angel, or He can speak to us directly. This in some ways is the most dangerous of all of the ways of guidance because all of these things are also counterfeited by Satan. Therefore, we must have a confirmation from another source to know that it is from God. We know that God spoke to Joseph (Mary's husband) through a dream. He spoke to many people in both the Old and New Testaments through angels, and frequently God has spoken directly to an individual, such as Moses or Paul. This type of guidance directly from God is usually much more rare than the previously mentioned types.

5. Peace in your heart: The final umpire, the final decider, the final ruler as to whether a particular plan of action that God seems to be indicating is really His will is whether or not you have peace in your heart. This is pointed out in Colossians 3:

15 And let the peace of Christ rule in your hearts, to which indeed you were called in one body; and be thankful.

No matter if a multitude of counselors are giving you direction in some area and the Bible seems to confirm it, if you do not have the perfect peace of God, do not proceed. We can use this in many ways.

I was speaking recently in Sioux Falls, South Dakota. A young lady came up to me, all in a dither, not knowing whether she and her husband should rent or buy a house. I told her that I sensed a total lack of peace in her, and I encouraged her to go pray and not to do anything until she had perfect peace from God.

In one of my books, I mentioned the example of Barney Coombs, who is now a pastor in Vancouver, B.C. At the time of this incident he was a pastor in England. He was driving home one night. The road to his house forked and later the two roads joined back together. Thus, he could take either the left fork or the right fork, with the time and distance being the same. He felt a strong urging to take the right fork. Most of us would have just done it without thinking. However, Barney prayed and said, "God if I am to take the right fork and this is of You, give me a real peace inside, and if not, give me a real disquiet." In answer to that prayer, God gave him a real disquiet, so he took the left fork instead. A little way down that road he picked up a hitchhiker whom he had the privilege of leading to Christ. Satan, in the worst way, did not want him to take the left fork, and thus was giving him a strong urge to take the right fork.

We can use this technique in our daily lives. When we have a decision to make that may seem inconsequential, such as whom to have lunch with, we can ask God:

"God, if you want me to have lunch with Joe, then give me a real peace inside and, if not, give me an unrest."

God delights in this kind of prayer and delights in answering us. People can have peace (of a sort) in their lives as long as they are not praying to God about the various decisions in their lives. Once they start praying and asking God not to let them have peace if they are not moving in His will, the peace will depart if God wants to redirect them. However, the peace will remain and increase if they are walking in His will.

Up until now we have just talked about guidance for an isolated individual. The same thing applies to more than one person. For example, if a husband and wife are both Christians, both seeking God's will, and are contemplating a particular action, I think God will give them both peace if it is His will for them to act in a certain manner. Similarly with a group of elders trying to arrive at a decision; if it is God's will, He will give them all perfect peace. What happens in a group of elders if four of them feel peace and the fifth one doesn't? In that situation one of two things is true:

1. It is not God's will that they take that particular action and He is using the fifth elder as a check to prevent them from making a mistake . . . or

2. The fifth elder has a spiritual problem that needs to be dealt with and is not hearing from God.

In either case I do not believe the action should be taken until there is perfect unity in the Spirit. It may be that the group needs to pause, deal with any spiritual problems among the elders and then reconsider the question. If everyone (or both people in a couple) does not feel perfect peace, either it is something that they should not do or at least one party is not truly seeking to do God's will, regardless of his own desires. Thus, God can use peace not only to direct individuals, but to direct groups of people as well. Thank you,

Lord for this beautiful and simple way that you let us know if we are walking in your will.

SUMMARY AND CONCLUSION

The one thing that God did not want us to have was the knowledge of good and evil. He knew that once we had it we would attempt to live independently of Him, making our own decisions based on our knowledge of good and evil, and we would no longer rely on Him, looking to Him for guidance on decisions. Once Adam and Eve gained this knowledge of good and evil, we can see that that is exactly what happened.

Through the ages, we have seen that knowing God and knowing good and evil are mutually exclusive. Our decisions are based either on our knowledge of good and evil or on what God says (God's will). Frequently, God's will or God's guidance is illogical and contrary to our knowledge of good and evil. We also discussed how we can know God's will.

If we are not careful, we can even use the Bible to make decisions independent of God. We can overemphasize the Ten Commandments and even make the New Testament a brand new law all in itself. Trying to be under the law and a set of rules and regulations is deadly, where having a personal, vital relationship with God the Father through Jesus Christ is alive and exciting.

We realize that there is another side to this question. We have only presented one side. But it seems that this is a basic, foundational truth in the Bible from beginning to end. We yearn that we and all of our readers would look to God for guidance and direction, and not to our own knowledge of good and evil.

This has been a difficult subject to address. Many will misunderstand and others will think I might be trying to rationalize something. With my whole heart I want to see people live righteous, holy lives and to obey and glorify our loving heavenly Father and His Son, Jesus Christ. I do not want to confuse, but only to help you draw closer to God. I believe that learning to look to God and to trust in Him, rather than relying on your knowledge of good and evil, will help you to do this.

MEET THE AUTHOR

Dr. James McKeever is an international consulting economist, lecturer, author, world traveler and Bible teacher. His financial consultations are utilized by scores of individuals from all over the world who seek his advice on investment strategy and international affairs.

Dr. McKeever is the editor and major contributing writer of the *McKeever Strategy Letter*, an economic and investment letter with worldwide circulation and recognition, rated #1 for 1985, 1986 and 1988 by an independent newsletter-rating service, and showing an average profit of 66.25 percent per year over the eleven year period 1978-1988.

Dr. McKeever has been a featured speaker at monetary, gold and tax haven conferences in London, Zurich, Bermuda, Amsterdam, South Africa, Australia, Singapore and Hong Kong, as well as all over the North American continent and Latin America.

As an economist and futurist, Dr. McKeever has shared the platform with such men as Ronald Reagan, Gerald Ford, William Simon, William Buckley, Alan Greenspan, heads of foreign governments and many other outstanding thinkers.

For five years after completing his academic work, Dr. McKeever was with a consulting firm which specialized in financial investments in petroleum. Those who were following his counsel back in 1954 invested heavily in oil.

For more than ten years he was with IBM, where he held several key management positions. During those years, when IBM was just moving into transistorized computers, he helped that company become what it is today. With IBM, he consulted with top executives of many major corporations in America, helping them solve financial, control and information problems. He has received many awards from IBM, including the "Key Man Award" and the "Outstanding Contribution Award." He is widely known in the computer field for his books and articles on management, management control and information sciences.

In addition to this outstanding business background, Dr. McKeever is an ordained minister. He has been a Baptist evangelist, pastor of Catalina Bible Church for three and a half years (while still with IBM) and a frequent speaker at Christian conferences. He has the gift of teaching and an indepth knowledge of the Bible, and has authored fourteen best-selling Christian books, seven of which have won the "Angel Award."

Dr. McKeever is president of Omega Ministries, which is a non-profit organization established under the leading of the Holy Spirit to minister to the body of Christ by the traveling ministry of anointed men of God, through books, cassettes, seminars, conferences and video tapes. He is the editor of the widely-read newsletter, *End-Times News Digest* (published by Omega Ministries), which relates the significance of current events to biblical prophecy and to the body of Christ today. The worldwide outreach of Omega Ministries is supported by the gifts of those who are interested.

WRITING TO THE AUTHOR

If this booklet, KNOWLEDGE OF GOOD AND EVIL, has made an impact on your life, you may want to write to Dr. McKeever in the space below.

Also, on the reverse side are shown some of his other materials and services.

Comments:

TO:
DR. JAMES McKEEVER
OMEGA MINISTRIES
P. O. BOX 4130
MEDFORD, OR 97501 USA

Dear Dr. McKeever,
I am enclosing:

☐ $_____ for additional copies of KNOWLEDGE OF
GOOD AND EVIL (for a contribution of $ each)

☐ $_____ for your ministry in general

☐ $_____ Total contribution enclosed
(make check payable to Omega Ministries)

☐ I will be praying for your ministry

NAME _____

ADDRESS _____

CITY _____

STATE _____ ZIP _____

PHONE _____

Also send me information on the following materials by Dr. James McKeever:

☐ Other booklets in this series
☐ The Christian newsletter that he edits, *End-Times News Digest (END)*
☐ Books by him
☐ Cassettes of his speaking ministry
☐ Information about his speaking at our church or Christian conference
☐ Please read comments on other side